My Story for His Glory

The Power of Prayer

SAMMIE DAVIS-DYSON

ISBN 978-1-0980-3805-2 (paperback)
ISBN 978-1-0980-3806-9 (hardcover)
ISBN 978-1-0980-3807-6 (digital)

Christian Faith Publishing, Inc.
832 Park Avenue
Meadville, PA 16335
www.christianfaithpublishing.com

Printed in the United States of America

Prelude

Though the stories included in this book are true, I want to make it clear that my marriage to Nathaniel Elliott Dyson had many good times. He loved me. I loved him. One of the several reasons that I loved him was that he was highly intelligent. He was creative and ingenious in ways in which he tried to keep a roof over our heads.

I loved him because he was compassionate, as demonstrated by many times he would befriend people who were downtrodden or not always accepted in "polite" society. I loved him because he was often generous with me; that is, he would buy me gifts that were practical and unique. To this day, I still have some of those gifts—one of which I use almost daily in the kitchen.

Nat loved to tell jokes and make people laugh. He was the "life of the party" when we would travel to visit his family, either in his birthplace in Sumter, South Carolina or siblings in New Jersey. He was one of several children of Henry and Janie Lee Dyson.

Because I was from Ohio, I missed living there during the couple years that Nat and I lived in New York. So, when I went home to Ohio to visit my parents, I told him that I really wanted to stay in Ohio and asked him if he could arrange to come to be with me. In short order, he made all the necessary arrangements and we began our residence together in Ohio.

Though you are going to read the truth of my life as you read the stories in this book, it is important to let you know that all was not horrible *all* the time! I will always have fond memories of such times. For example, when I was a choir member at Church of the Open Door, I was so proud of seeing Nat walking down the aisle because he was one of the ushers passing the plates among the pews during offering time. He was a sharp dresser, and I loved seeing him looking so handsome!

During the spans of time when he was sober, he was a good husband. He tried to be—and often succeeded at being—a good father. He always wanted the very best for his children.

Neither he nor I wanted to make any differentiation between the children he and I had together, versus the three that were from his first marriage. That was a rule that he and I fully agreed on and embraced.

I suppose that I may have stayed married to Nathaniel if I had been raised in a home where any kinds of addictions existed, but I wasn't. The closest I came to know what that kind of a life was like was in the fact that my mother's son (but not my father's) was an alcoholic. He ultimately died of cirrhosis of the liver. I witnessed what delirium tremens looked and sounded like, commonly known as "the D.T.'s". Seeing that scared me!

Anyway, to emphasize that I knew there was quite a bit that was positive about the true heart of Nat, I remarried him in 1991, after having divorced him in 1978. He died in 1995 as the result of yet another heart attack. He had open heart surgery in 1976 and a second one in 1986. Between those two Cleveland Clinic surgeries, he had many heart attacks. In fact, I quit counting after heart attack #13. By the time we remarried, he had also had a stroke, adding insult to injury, in terms of his weakening health.

His death in 1995 was discovered by a pedestrian in the Bronx, New York. Nat had stopped there—probably to visit a friend he knew—prior to moving on to Yale University in New Haven, Connecticut to pick up our youngest child, our son. The pedestrian had noticed that a vehicle's motor had been running when she had walked past its parking spot the day before and noticed that the motor was still running the next day in the same parking spot. She saw no one inside.

Our son had called me 24 hours after his father had left Ohio and inquired where his daddy was. That phone call resulted in Nat's body being ultimately discovered on the floor of the vehicle after he had passed away four days prior!

The reality of living in a fallen world that has been that way ever since Adam and Eve disobeyed God's command for obedience, is a reality that has made relationships difficult in all instances. Of course, some are more successful than others because they are more compatible than others—on several levels. But even the most successful relationships are successful because of the hard work of compromise, patience, camaraderie, mutual support of one another, respect for one another, and a mutual desire to walk in obedience to the counsel of the Holy Spirit.

I ask that you keep these words in mind as you read the excerpts of my life journey contained herein. I wasn't married to a monster. I was married to a man suffering from his own deep pain left over from his childhood. Sadly, his marriage and children suffered the consequences of his pain.

My parents, Arthur and Emma Lou Davis, were fine role models for me and my three brothers. They modeled honesty, compassion, moral integrity, persistence in work, and general all-around Christian principles. They were quite strict. Of course, as children, my brothers and I did not appreciate the strictness. Later in life, we came to understand and appreciate having had these tight boundaries. It made it easier later in our lives to know what to discard and what to retain as our life rules. That was easier for us to do than it would have been to know the difference between right and wrong if we had not been raised with rules and boundaries.

The persistence and perseverance that I am blessed with is credited to them. They did not give up or throw in the towel during times of struggle. Though they had little in terms of formal education (Daddy had even less than Mom), they made the very most of self-learning. Daddy built our first house and he was so very proud of the work of his hands!

Daddy was very intelligent. In spite of very little formal schooling, he spent long hours studying at the library. He spent long hours studying the Bible. He became pastor of a church in Tennessee and later in Ohio. The congregation learned from his teachings, especially given the backgrounds from which the majority of those dear people had come.

To conclude this important prelude, it is important to all my children that I give credit to where it is due, on behalf of their father. It was also important to give credit to the parents who raised me.

The goal of this book is to give hope to the reader that *prayer works!* But the intent is not to throw anyone "under the bus". It is also my goal to show that all ultimate credit is to be given to the Holy Spirit, and not myself. It often has taken prodding and pushing before I *finally* obeyed and only then was when I reaped the benefits of obedience.

Preface

It has not been possible to write this story of the history and impact of prayer in my life without also including certain personal details of my life. However, the most extremely personal details have been omitted. I am most interested in the privacy, confidentiality, and well-being of those people whom I love dearly. Pseudonyms are used when it has been necessary to use names.

I have been told for decades that I should write a book about my life's amazing turns from the better to the worse and back to the better. I decided it is time to do so. I suppose this book can be considered a handbook of sorts. It is written in sections, chronologically, with appropriate Scriptures heading each section.

Though I find much utility in several Bible translations, I memorized Scripture as a child and a teen in the poetic old Shakespearean dialect of the King James version of the Bible. It is from that background of childhood memorization that the quotes herein are obtained.

United Airlines Reservationist, 1967

Occupy until I come. (Work, have an occupation.)

—Luke 19:13

I graduated from Midview High School in 1962 at seventeen years old. My first job—beyond babysitting—was working as a sanitation dishwasher in the laboratory of Elyria Memorial Hospital. It was my job to clean the glassware used for doing various lab tests from patients. I did that until I got my first *big* break by being hired by United Airlines, working as a reservationist in 1967.

I started at an entry income of $440 a month! In 1967, that was equivalent to at least five or six times that amount now! I bought myself a new blue 1967 Pontiac Grand Prix convertible. I was *so* proud of that car! My parents were *so* proud of me!

This was the result of persistency in school from first grade to graduation. This was the result of persistency in the job world, not giving up when the job at Elyria Memorial Hospital was not the greatest in the world. This was the result of asking the Lord to please give me the next good job.

Working for United Airlines was fun and carried its privileges. I could fly from here to the west coast for only $8, or less than that if I flew closer to home than that. I transferred to the New York office of United in, perhaps, 1968 and stayed with them until I left to return to Ohio in 1970 but, then, worked again at the Cleveland location until 1972.

I had met my husband in New York when I was visiting my older sister (actually, my father's daughter from his first marriage) who was dealing with breast cancer, and he was renting a room from her in her boarding house. It was a Saturday as my sister and I were having a conversation in her kitchen. He had to walk through the kitchen of her boarding house in order to go to his private space at the back of the house that he was renting from her.

I was struck by his intellect and his eloquence of speech. I was struck by the fancy attire he was wearing that night, as he was prepared to go out on the town, it seemed. My sister introduced us, and that was the beginning of his interest in me. When I arrived back home to Ohio after being with my sister, she called me and said that Nat was very interested in me. He wanted permission to call me. I told my sister that he could. He did. He invited to fly me back to New York and to lodge me at the New York Hilton. He was making good money as an HVAC/R journeyman, so he could afford it.

I was struck by the great first date he took me on which was to a Manhattan dinner theater to see the Count Basie band! I was further struck by his classiness in terms of cuisine. I was later struck by his own cooking skills. He taught me a lot about cooking. Props to my mother also; however, until I met Nathaniel Elliott Dyson, I had avoided the kitchen in spite of my mother's best efforts to get me interested. I preferred cleaning the house and keeping it orderly. I still love doing that, but I also learned to love cooking.

This portion of my story is much less about prayer and much more about simply connecting more of the dots of my life and history, I must admit. It is a necessary connective introduction.

Prayer Produced a Bicycle and Breakfast, 1971

Ask and it shall be given you, seek and ye shall find,
knock, and it shall be opened unto you

—Matthew 7:7

Among my early memories of the power of prayer in my life, it was around 1971. I had five children at the time, and one had not been born yet. (I will explain later how I already had five children but had only known Nat about three years at that point). Anyway, the sixth child would be born in July 1973.

It was a Saturday morning in 1971 and time for breakfast. The children were seated around the breakfast table, awaiting their food. I was alone in the kitchen. Nat was very seldom home on weekends due to drinking and gambling addictions. (I had seen the clear "red flag" before that fancy first date that he had taken me on to see Count Basie. Nat had been more than an hour late arriving to pick me up. I learned much later that his tardiness was due to playing poker in order to get enough money to treat me in highest fashion that night).

Back to the Saturday morning in 1971, the children were seated at the table, asking me when breakfast would be ready. I was alone in the kitchen, asking God to supply breakfast for us while trying to assure the children that I was "working on it." Due to my husband's addictions, there was seldom enough money to take care of groceries and other needs. Nat would not only lose his paycheck at the poker table but would come home in the wee hours of the night and demand my paycheck. I couldn't just say no because I would get terrorized or even hit.

On that particular Saturday morning, there were two items in the refrigerator—a jar of water and a jar of pickles. The previous night's dinner had used up all of what was left of the potatoes, from which I created a delicious dish that the kids loved. But now, I was hard-pressed to figure out how to make breakfast out of water and pickles.

So I stood there in the kitchen and silently but fervently prayed. I asked God for a miracle. It was not very long after I said amen when there was a knock on the backdoor leading into the kitchen. It was a neighbor's son who lived across the street. He was about ten years old. He said that he was wondering if he could buy the bicycle that had been laying in the front yard of the house. It had been lying where my oldest son of my husband's first marriage had basically abandoned it days before because it was old and rusty. Of the five children, three were from my husband's first marriage, but I seldom refer to them as stepchildren. They immediately became my children when we rescued them from very dire straits at ages twelve, eight, and seven.

Anyway, about the bike in the yard, I told the neighbor kid, whose name was Wesley, that the bicycle he was interested in was old and somewhat rusted out. I told him that he would likely not be interested in the bike if he took a closer look at it. He responded that he had already done so and that it was a very nice bike, and he really wanted to buy it from me.

At that point, I said, "Wesley, I think you should go ask your mother if she thinks it is worth buying."

A few minutes later, he was back with $10 and a smile, stating that his mother believed it was well worth that amount which had been his original suggestion, not mine, because I didn't expect him to actually buy it. In 1971, $10 was more like $50, or more, in today's money! So I walked up the street to the convenience store and bought an entire week's worth of groceries! As the Scripture at the beginning of this story indicated, I had asked, I had sought, and there was a knock on my back door that Saturday morning!

Pills, Pilot Light, and Razors
An Unexpected Encounter, 1972

The steps of a good man are ordered by the
Lord, and he delighteth in his way.

—Psalms 37:23

The Elyria house we had been living in when we rescued the children from their rather pitiful living conditions in South Carolina had been foreclosed only after a couple years or less of living there, due to the addictions of my husband. After living for a few short weeks with my parents, we found an LMHA apartment in South Park Apartments in Elyria. One day, one of my children came to me while I was working in the kitchen and said that an ambulance had come to the apartment building behind ours and had taken one of its residents to the hospital because she had tried to commit suicide. She lived in building D, and we lived in building C. She had been discovered in her apartment with her wrists slit, an empty pill bottle on the floor beside her, and the apartment smelling of gas because she had turned off the pilot light of the gas stove.

My son told me that her name was Rosa Johnson and that she had three young daughters as a single mom. I had never met Rosa and did not even know what she looked like. Further, I had never met anyone who had tried to take their own life. As a result, I didn't see any point in getting involved.

A couple of days went by, and each night, I had trouble sleeping. Holy Spirit also took my appetite. He told me why this was happening. It was because he wanted me to go to the hospital and witness to Rosa. I disobeyed for a couple of days. After all, I did not know her, and her situation of being suicidal scared and intimidated me. What would I look like, paying a visit to someone whom I did not know and who may be in no mood to see a stranger walking into her hospital room?

Holy Spirit wouldn't stop "bugging" me though. Finally, because I was tired of not sleeping or eating, I yielded, picked up my Bible, and thought of some verses that I might be able to share with Rosa if she would allow me to do so. I arrived at the door of her room at Elyria Memorial Hospital and, with shaky knees, walked in. I saw the face of an angry and cold young woman. After I introduced myself and told her where I lived and how I knew about her, I asked for just a few moments of her time because I wanted to just give her some words of hope.

She granted me that opportunity. I certainly do not remember exactly what I said nor do I remember if whatever I said included any sharing of Scripture. What I do remember is that as I was thanking her for her time, she stated she would be discharged the following day and asked if I would mind coming over for a visit that evening. She said she wanted to ask me some questions about God.

Of course, I agreed and accepted her invitation. That night, she plowed me with questions, and I opened up Scripture after Scripture for her. One of the statements she made was that she believed in evolution, not in God. Calmly, I asked her to consider these questions, "If evolution says that we come from apes, why are apes still being born and human babies still being born?" "Wouldn't apes no longer exist, now that humans do? And if there was a 'big bang' that brought the universe into being, where did the elements that caused the 'big bang' come from?" and "Did they create themselves?"

By the time much Scripture was shared, and Rosa contemplated what she was hearing, I could tell that she was receptive, so I asked her if she wanted the peace of God in her life by accepting Jesus as her Savior. She said yes. I led her in the sinner's prayer, and she was immediately different in her appearance. I saw her smile for the first time since we had met, perhaps thirty-six hours earlier!

Within perhaps merely weeks from that night, she and her little daughters moved from that apartment complex to the city of Lorain. I did not see her a whole lot after that, but I did see her maybe twice over the years. She always had a big smile, told me that she was involved in a church, and thanked me for leading her to Christ! I, too, had a smile on my face because there was peace in my heart that had come from obedience to the call of the Holy Spirit! Well, *eventual* obedience, that is. He had truly ordered my steps that day in spite of having to drag me into submission and obedience!

The Lawyer, His Request,
My Refusal, 1975

Lying lips (are) abomination to the LORD: but
they that deal truly (are) his delight.

—Proverbs 12:22

I received a position as a legal secretary to an attorney in downtown Elyria in 1975. All went well until one day, he asked me to tell certain clients who might call on the phone that he was not there. He was there, but he gave me instructions to tell them he was out of the office. I was raised very strictly. My pastor father told us children never to lie. I never heard him lie. I never heard my mother lie.

The next day, I asked my attorney boss if I could speak with him for just a moment. He stopped his work and listened as I told him that I was sorry, but I wouldn't be able to lie for him when clients might call. He fired me right then, so I left.

Then I started praying, asking God to guide me to what was next. I did not like receiving government assistance, so I found my next job, working as a clerk-typist for Lorain County Children Services, but the job did not last beyond a few years. It was then that I obtained a temporary position at Allen Memorial Hospital that was supposed to be for six weeks to cover the medical leave of the executive secretary to the director of the hospital, J.C. Palin.

Even though my truthfulness with the attorney had gotten me fired (or perhaps because of that truthfulness), each subsequent position paid a bit better and better, including this one at Allen Memorial Hospital. However, it was not a *lot* better. Yet my prayers kept being answered. I guess, as the Scripture at the beginning of this story about lying indicated, the Lord had found delight in me for not lying.

Wilkes Villa Riot, Shooting, and Prayer, 1975

A thousand shall fall at thy side, and ten thousand at thy right hand; but it shall not come nigh thee.

—Psalms 91:7

A police shooting of a Black man had taken place in Elyria. Some members of the Black community were up in arms. Literally. They became armed with guns. They began to loot grocery stores. One night, a shooting broke out in Wilkes Villa as a car filled with looted grocery items—mostly meats—arrived into the village. I do not clearly remember, but I think the fight broke out over the desire for the various kinds of meats.

What I do clearly remember is praying fervently for the safety of my children. I cautioned the older ones to get down low to the floor so that they could avoid getting hit by any flying bullets that might come through the window. I remember lying on top of the youngest two children so that I could take any potential hit but save them from being shot. I prayed and had my children lie down as still is possible. Finally, it was over. No one was shot. Prayer was answered. The bullets had not come near us.

How Prayer Got Me to the City of Oberlin, 1977

For I know the plans I have for you, declares the Lord;
plans to prosper you and not to harm you, plans
to give you (a) hope, and a future.

—Jeremiah 29:11

After a couple years living in the South Park apartment complex, we moved about a mile away to the projects called Wilkes Villa. I do not remember why. It was certainly no improvement, just "frying pan into the fire." My phone rang, one day, during my years of residing there in Wilkes Villa. It was the Lorain Metropolitan Housing Authority (LMHA). The lady said that they had an empty unit in Oberlin with four bedrooms. My family of six children and my husband and I certainly qualified for four bedrooms.

She said that she decided to call me because she wanted some good, clean, and orderly tenants to occupy the unit because she said that Oberlin was a nice town, and she did not want rowdy people there who would embarrass LMHA. I had always been attracted to the art, music, and culture of Oberlin. Of course, I was also aware of its quirky idiosyncrasies, but that was not really negative or as important as all that appealed to me, including the friendliness and acceptance of its citizens.

When we moved there, I very soon received an invitation from the Oberlin Welcome Wagon organization. I was invited to a dinner that involved eating courses at different homes as a way of meeting those residents. I forget the name of the dinner experience, so I shall call it the traveling dinner. Hors d'oeuvres were at the first home, salad (or was it soup, or both?) at the second, main course at the third, and dessert rounded out the experience at the fourth home. I thought how nice it was for the city to welcome me, a new resident who was also an LMHA tenant!

This whole improvement in my and my family's living conditions was definitely the beginning of something wonderful to come! It was the beginning of my Oberlin future! The steps of a good person are ordered by the Lord! He knew the plans he had for me which were to prosper me and not to harm me, to give me a future and a hope!

This change happened as the result of the desires of my heart being answered. I do not literally remember praying my way out of Wilkes Villa, but I definitely remember *wishing* my way out. I will not take prayer credit where prayer credit is not due.

Prayer Produced a Sheriff with His Own Gas Pump, 1980

Trust in the Lord with all thine heart;
lean not unto thine own understanding. In all thy ways
acknowledge him and he will direct thy paths.

—Proverbs 3:5–6

I had been seeing commercials on television over the course of several days, advertising that the Barnum & Bailey Circus was coming to the Richfield Coliseum in Richfield, Ohio. Some of you reading this may remember when it existed. I wanted so badly to take the children. At that point, there were only my biological three children because the two remaining older ones had been taken back to South Carolina by their father when I divorced him in 1978 due to his addictions that had ruined our marriage.

The oldest of those three children had been killed by hitchhikers when he was eighteen years old in 1977. This was the same son whose bicycle had been bought by Wesley in 1971. Anyway, in 1977, my son was driving home from Parris Island, South Carolina, Marine Corps basic training. He was coming home because I had written him a letter telling him that I was going to have to divorce his father because the pressure was so bad that I was broken out in hives from head to toe, and I just couldn't take it anymore. My son had begged me not to do so, at least not until he could get permission to come home and talk to me. He said that I had been the only really good mother that he had ever had, and he did not want to lose me.

As he was on his way home, he picked up those three hitchhikers. They decided they wanted his vehicle and could dispense with him, so they shot him and left his body in a supermarket parking lot to be discovered the next day.

Now back to the story about the circus to which I wanted to take the children in October of 1980. I was on public assistance at that time, so I saved and saved until I had enough money to take the children and enough money for about a half-tank of gas. Though I lived in Oberlin, I knew I could get to Richfield and back home on half a tank. We enjoyed the circus, and I enjoyed seeing the children have a great time. They were ages ten, nine, and seven, which were perfect ages for such an event! But then, on the way home, I got lost. Very lost. I ran extremely low on gas.

At that point, it was no longer the daylight of an afternoon. It was the darkness of night. My children had fallen asleep in the back seat. I prayed and asked God to send perhaps a state trooper along to help me. I decided that the thing to do would be to pull off the shoulder of the highway of Interstate 77 south and raise the hood of the car so a state trooper would see me and maybe put enough gas in the car for me to get home. I had no money left. I had used it to put the half-tank of gas into the car earlier that day before leaving Oberlin. So to me, it was common sense to pull off onto the shoulder of the highway and wait and pray for a trooper to show up.

However, God had a different plan for me, so His Holy Spirit began telling me not to pull off into the shoulder of the highway but to get off at the next exit. I argued with this "voice"—this urging in my spirit. I said that was a "stupid" idea because there would be far less likelihood of getting help with my plight if I pulled off onto some street where I stood little chance of getting help. The urging of the Holy Spirit within me was relentless. So I reluctantly obeyed and took the next exit. My car drifted to a stop soon thereafter. It was completely out of gas. The place that it stopped was directly in front of a white house that had a sidewalk leading from the front of the house directly to the front passenger-side door of my car.

My children were still asleep. I sat there behind the wheel and prayed and, then, got out of the car and walked up that long sidewalk and knocked on the door of that house. I didn't know what else to do. I fully expected that no one would open the door, especially if the door had a peephole, and the person could see a Black female stranger standing there. But the tall White man opened the door and listened to me tell him my plight. With a smile, he introduced himself as the sheriff of the little village called Nova, Ohio. To this very day, I do *not* know how in the world I ended up *there* from Richfield! The tall kind man with the smile said, "You are at the right place for something like this to happen. I happen to have an in-ground gas pump in my backyard. I will go get my gas can and put enough in your car so that I can drive it back there and fill it up. Meantime, get your children out and bring them inside to warm up. My wife will be happy to give you all some hot chocolate." Wow!

When it was all taken care of, I asked them for their name and address because I told them that as soon as I could, I would send them payment for the cost of a full tank of gas. They declined. I insisted. They relented. I drove home without getting lost again, all the while being in absolute awe of what God had just done! I mailed them a check for $10 a few weeks later. This was *no* luck; this was God!

Were these people angels? "Be not forgetful to entertain strangers: for thereby some have entertained angels unawares" (Hebrews 13:2). Do angels entertain strangers though? I didn't entertain them. They entertained *me*! They entertained *us*!

Hot Meals, a Caring Church, and Daily Walks During a Portion of the 1980s

*Trust in the Lord, and do good; so shalt thou dwell in the land,
and verily thou shalt be fed. Delight thyself (also) in the Lord:
and he shall give thee the desires of thine heart. Commit thy way
unto the Lord; trust also in him; and he shall bring it to pass.*

—Psalms 37:3–5

There were varying spans of time during the 1980s when I did not know where the next meal was coming from. Those were times between jobs. Those were times where my children and I relied heavily on the goodness of the hearts of others. There were many trips to the Salvation Army or Goodwill. There were many embarrassing trips to the grocery store where I had to pay with physical food stamps, not like these days where one uses a card that could appear to be a debit or credit card.

At one point during that time—even with the food stamps—there was not enough to cover the cost of feeding myself and three children for a whole month. So once again, I prayed for sustenance. You see, I had told my children, one day when we saw a local newscast, that there will never be an excuse for anyone of us to steal food or anything else. I had said that because the news story had been about a man who had been caught shoplifting from a grocery store, and he said that it was because he needed to feed his family. I used that teaching moment to let my children know that even if things got so rough that we needed to go to neighbors' houses and ask for a "cup of this or a can of that," we would do so, but we would not steal anything ever!

So I had noticed a church on South Main Street in Oberlin that served hot meals daily. It is called Christ Episcopal Church, and it was within walking distance of my LMHA house. So every day, the children and I would walk to that church for dinner. It was so embarrassing, but my daughter had an ingenious idea. She asked the servers if she could assist them, and they allowed her to do so in order for it to appear that she was a volunteer there, not just a poor person coming for handouts. I was proud of her for that. She has always been creative that way and still is, though, thankfully, not for the same reasons.

During the weekends, when hot meals are not served, we ate cereal. My parents loaned me enough money for that, and I always paid them back when I received my monthly welfare check. They knew they could trust me, and I never let them down. After all, their hearts were breaking for the plight that I had gotten myself into many years earlier by having married a man whom I later found out was seriously addicted to alcohol and gambling. At this point, he and I had been divorced for several years, but things had been no better than when we had been married. In fact, they had been worse. At least, at this point in time when it was just me and the children, I could have the peace of mind of having less drama in my and my children's lives.

Prayer Guided My Steps
into College, 1985

The steps of a good man are ordered by the
Lord, and he delighteth in his way.

—Psalms 37:23

It was 1985. I was in a conversation with a coworker at Allen Memorial Hospital where I had worked since 1978. (The six-week temp assignment mentioned in a previous story had turned into an eventual eight years). The discussion centered around a recent heartbreak I was feeling, based on the breakup of a romantic relationship. This relationship had been perhaps a few months long and had happened during the more than twelve-year time span between my 1978 divorce and my eventual 1991 remarriage to the children's father—my husband. I had been told by one of his daughters (mine also, as far as love goes) that her father had become clean and sober and read his Bible a lot. That was music to my ears. He had tried and tried over those twelve-plus years to get me to agree to get back together.

Anyway, during that talk with my coworker in 1985, she mentioned three things that she said I would do well to consider, in order to focus on doing something for me, rather than wallowing in my sorrow over the recently lost romantic relationship. She mentioned three ideas or suggestions. I have long forgotten two of them, but the third one was that perhaps I should consider going "back" to school. I responded that her suggestion could not apply to me because I could not go "back" to college because I had never even begun college because even though I had always wanted to go to college, I simply could not afford it.

Further, I told her the only college I could go to would have to be Oberlin because that would be the only one that I could walk to due to not having or being able to afford to buy a car. So that was how that conversation concluded.

A year passed after that conversation between the coworker and me. As always, I was walking across the campus of Oberlin College on my way home from work at the hospital at the end of the day. I still did not own a car which had been the case for ultimately a total of seven years. I was talking to the Lord as I walked across campus as I looked longingly at those beautiful historic buildings and those very fortunate students who were part of that world. I *knew* I could never be a part of such a privilege, so I continued walking toward my Lorain Metropolitan Housing Authority home.

But God spoke to me as I was walking, wishing, and praying about wanting to be blessed enough to go to college but, at the same time, thanking him for the job I had at the hospital. It was a lot better than many friends my age had. I was especially thanking Him for the fact that I hadn't been expected to work at the hospital any more than six weeks. I had been sent there by a temporary agency to cover for the executive secretary while she was out on medical leave. She was the executive secretary to the man who was the director of the hospital. When she returned, I was soon transferred to the hospital laboratory because the director of the lab wanted me to become one of the two laboratory secretaries. So six weeks eventually became eight years.

So as I was walking across the college campus in 1986, the Holy Spirit prompted me to ask the next student who would come across my path how to get to the financial aid office. What? Why would I do that? I couldn't even afford a car, let alone the cost of education at a world-renowned, expensive private college! But the Spirit's prompting was strong within me.

So the next student to come across my path directed me to the building and the floor of the building where I could find the financial aid office. I asked to speak to the director. I learned that his name was James White, but the man who came to the counter to greet me was not James White. He was the assistant director, Ross Peacock, who told me that Mr. White was out of town at a conference, but Mr. Peacock asked if he could help me.

I began by apologizing for just showing up without an appointment but told him that I wanted to become a college student but that I had no money and no car, so Oberlin would be the only college that I could get to. I told Mr. Peacock that I had always wanted a college education so that I could become a counselor or psychologist. I went on to tell him that I had heard of something called financial aid, but I had believed that meant that the student had to have the majority of the money, and the college would fill in any small gap to complete the total amount needed. So once my five- to seven-minute spiel was over, I once again apologized for just showing up and then I turned to leave.

Just as my hand was on the doorknob to leave, Mr. Peacock said, "Wait, come back!"

He sounded friendly, and he had not snickered, rolled his eyes, or interrupted my "I want to go to college, but I'm too broke to go anywhere else but here because I don't have a car to get anywhere else" spiel.

So now, I'm standing back at the counter, and he is still looking at me pleasantly. I thought to myself, *He doesn't really understand what I meant when I said I have no money*, so I expressed those words out loud. Then, he said, "I know. I heard you the first time, but you strike me as the kind of person who, if we were to underwrite your education, you would not let us down."

I blurted out, "Oh no, sir, I would definitely not let you down!"

Then he directed me to the building that housed the admissions office and told me to head over there. He said he would call them and tell them a little about me, and he was sure they would get some paperwork started. Then, he told me that I was to return to him, and he would get some paperwork started. They did. He did.

A few months later, after jumping through several admissions requirements (application, scholastic aptitude testing, essay writing, etc.), I received a letter in the mail welcoming me as a member of the class of 1990! *Only* God gets credit for that because even though my high school GPA was not awful, it was nowhere near a 4.0!

Wow! Though there is much more to this new journey that began with a 1985 conversation between me and a hospital coworker, this actually began with a conversation between me and the Lord as I walked across campus and his Holy Spirit told me to ask a student where to find the financial aid office. "Trust in the Lord with all your heart; lean not on your own understanding. In all your ways acknowledge him and he will direct your paths" (Proverbs 3:5–6).

The Oberlin Prayer Story
Continues on Campus, 1993

The effectual, fervent prayer of a righteous man
(person) availeth much.

—James 5:16

I had experienced a glorious commencement day in 1990, receiving a standing ovation from the crowd of hundreds, amid the clicking camera lenses of photographers from three local newspapers: Oberlin News-Tribune, Elyria Chronicle-Telegram, and Lorain Morning Journal. Now, three years had passed, and it was 1993. My psychology and religion majors had not translated into a lucrative career in either field, so my income had been meager and mediocre, doing everything from selling Kirby vacuum cleaners door-to-door and then working in retail sales at J.C. Penney and then, at some point, adding a concurrent gig of working as an in-home parent-infant enrichment coordinator, working for the PIE (parent-infant enrichment) program.

I did have a brief temp agency job as a secretary for the summer of 1990 at Lorain County Community College, working for the director of institutional development. I had enjoyed that.

That aside, I decided to talk to the Lord about the fact that I was not really happy with these pieces and parts of jobs, *most* of them not really fulfilling. I asked Him to provide a means of income that would feel much more like a career, not merely just a job.

The phone rang after a period of perhaps weeks of praying had passed. It was Oberlin College. They told me they had been trying to reach me for a while because they had created two new almost identical positions, and they felt that I was the perfect candidate to apply for one of them. The position was called special advisor, located in the department of student academic services. The requirements were working with first-year, first-generation, and low-income students. After I was hired, my position was renamed coordinator of special advising. This change meant that I was now in charge of programming as the major focus of the position. I was chosen, in part, because I had been from those same first-generation, low-income demographics as an Oberlin student. I had experienced the disorientation and culture shock of being among students who were wealthy, well-traveled, and could write a check for the entire education without blinking an eye. So of course, I was tailor-made for the position of coordinator of special advising, as became renamed from Special Advisor after I was hired.

This meant that I was to interview, hire, and train students who were in their junior or senior year and who were of the same demographic as the students targeted for our program. Once hired, I was to oversee their training over the course of each semester that was designed for each of the seven of them to serve as mentors (known as peer liaisons) to about fifteen to twenty-five students each. These fifteen to twenty-five students assigned to each peer liaison were in their first year. The peer liaisons' job was that of helping those students become oriented and acclimated to the culture and academic rigor of the college.

I was absolutely in love with this job. Now, I had a career—not just a job! I would often mentally pinch myself about the reality of what prayer had yielded in my life! All those years of walking across campus, wishing or daydreaming about how fortunate the students were who went there. About how they must be so smart and so rich. About how wonderful the architecture of the buildings was and how fortunate were those employed there. About how impossible it would be for a person like me who had a long history of living in public housing units to ever be able to work for such a renowned college.

After all, I had lived in the projects of South Park and Wilkes Villa for a few years. So why in the world would Oberlin want me?

But the following story is about me praying under that stairwell inside Mudd Library that July or August in 1993 was fervent indeed, and God caused it to be effective indeed. It made much available to me for the next fifteen years of my awestruck life!

Prayer Under the Stairs in Mudd Library, 1993

*Delight thyself also in the Lord: and he shall
give thee the desires of thine heart.*

—Psalms 37:4

When I received that phone call in 1993 requesting that I apply for one of two positions at Oberlin in the department of student academic services, which I mentioned above, I needed to fill in a couple of prehire details. I almost did *not* get the job. One of the members of the search committee did not want me to be hired. His wife was the supervisor of the PIE program mentioned earlier. One day, she had seen me working at J.C. Penney during a portion of the hours that I was to be on the clock for PIE, visiting with young mothers in their homes. The job required spending afternoons in the homes of young single mothers under the age of twenty-one, where I would spend an hour teaching them parenting skills with their child or children.

I always kept those appointments with those mothers, but sometimes, I would arrange with them to meet in the evenings or on weekends. This would allow me to accommodate the J.C. Penney work hours while still keeping true to my job required of me in the PIE program. Well, when the PIE supervisor came into the J.C. Penney store and saw me, she fired me on the spot. Of course, I understand how that looked to her. I was also aware of the fact that even though it looked like I was cheating PIE, I knew I wasn't.

I explained this scenario to the bureau of unemployment, and they accepted my explanation and, in turn, required PIE to pay for my fifty-two weeks of unemployment. The member of the Oberlin search committee who was the husband of my PIE supervisor was very angry that his wife's organization had been ordered to pay my unemployment expenses, so that is why he did not want me to be hired for the Oberlin position.

When the dean of the department of student academic services that wanted to hire me asked me to explain to him why this particular member of the search team did not want me hired, I told the dean the whole story. At that point, he suggested that I return after lunch at 1:00 p.m., which would give him an opportunity to think through this dilemma.

During that period of perhaps about two hours, I looked for a private place to pray about this critical matter. I finally found a spot under the stairwell of the library located in the center of campus called Mudd Library, named after a prominent Oberlin alum, Seeley G. Mudd. I knelt down under the stairwell out of the view of pass-ersby and fervently prayed for the job. I fervently prayed for most of that couple of hours.

Upon arriving back at Dean Patrick Penn's office, he told me that he would hire me for the position of special advisor. The name of the position was soon changed to coordinator of special advising. I began in August 1993 and stayed until retiring in 2008. I retired in order to take a job that I had obtained at Lorain County Community College (LCCC).

You see, even though I was very happy with my Oberlin job, I was also desirous of what, for me, would be an even more exciting and rewarding job. That job would be to become a college professor, full-time. I knew that would never happen at Oberlin for several reasons; the most obvious of which was that I had no PhD.

Prayer, My Job Application on a Windowsill, and a Phone Call, 2004

Be careful (anxious/worried) for nothing, but in everything by prayer and supplication with thanksgiving, let your requests be made known unto God. And the peace of God which passes all understanding shall keep your hearts and minds through Christ Jesus.

—Philippians 4:6–7

Delight thyself also in the Lord: and he shall give thee the desires of thine heart.

—Psalms 37:4

The administrative associate in the division of social sciences and human services at LCCC called me during a workday at Oberlin in 2004. She knew me from the summer of 1990 when I had worked at LCCC through a temporary employment agency, and I had made several friendships during that brief time.

During that 2004 phone call, she said the dean, James Toman, affectionately known as JT, had been cleaning his office that day and saw a packet of paper lying on his windowsill. He discovered it was a "stray" job application from a Sammie Davis-Dyson. Upon reading it, he asked his administrative associate to call me. I had completed the application nine years earlier in 1995 after I earned my Master of Education degree from Cleveland State University in May of that year. In 1998, I also earned an education specialist degree from CSU, which is a degree in psychometrics, which is the art and science of administering intelligence, career, personality, and psychological assessments.

I had given up hope of ever being hired for the coveted position of teaching psychology either in a full-time capacity or as an adjunct (part-time) professor, partly because of not having a PhD or other doctoral degree.

In spite of that, I was asked to interview for the position of adjunct professor of psychology. JT hired me after only one interview. There was no search committee involved because this had not been for a fulltime position, and it also had not been for an advertised position. The Lord wanted me to have the job of my dreams, so he placed the application on the windowsill. He was orchestrating the whole process.

I started the job in August 2004 and am still doing it to this day. Can I say that I prayed for this opportunity? No, I cannot say for sure that I did. What I can say for sure is that I desired it with all my heart.

Interestingly, I worked at Oberlin until I retired in 2008, but I had begun teaching at LCCC in 2004. My Oberlin supervisor had allowed me to drive to LCCC to teach a class over the one-and-a-half-hour lunch break, and I also taught evening classes after the Oberlin workday.

I retired from Oberlin in 2008 because LCCC had advertised a full-time position as professor of counseling, tenure track. I was hired for it. I also continued to teach psychology, especially when I found out that this new full-time position was not an actual teaching position but, rather, a type of hybrid position that consisted of counseling students to help them most efficiently get through their academic journey. It required all the obligations of a teaching professor except I was not teaching. That is why I kept the part-time teaching position. My greatest career joy of all career joys is teaching.

I have been a Bible teacher since I was eleven years old, teaching little children in Sunday school. My pastor-father was a great teacher. I inherited his teaching genes. I expanded my theological and biblical knowledge over the decades to the point that I taught theological, prophetic, and exegetical scriptural topics at Oberlin from the mid-1990s to the mid-2010s in Oberlin's special program called experimental college (EXCO). This is a nonpaid opportunity for anyone to teach in an area of expertise that they really enjoy and would bring knowledge to the students. A graduation requirement for Oberlin students is they must take two of these EXCO courses during the course of their four years. One of my majors from Oberlin had been religion, not just psychology. However, I stopped teaching EXCO in 2015, partly due to my tight schedule.

I retired from the professor of counseling job at LCCC in 2014, simply because the requirements of a full-time professor position are grueling. Not the teaching/student-counseling part, of which I did the latter, but rather because of all the committee duties and other peripheral stuff loosely connected with the job.

Prayer Scared the Demons Away in the Decade of the 2000s

And these signs shall follow them that believe; in my name they shall cast out devils (demons).

—Mark 16:17a

Sometimes, praying is scary. I can testify to two such occasions when I would have been happy to "volunteer" someone else for the job that the Holy Spirit thrust upon me and not onto someone else. It was perhaps around the year 2000 when my ex-daughter-in-law who is the mother of my two oldest grandsons called me and asked me to please come and get rid of the forces of darkness in her apartment. Things had gotten so dark and scary that she had taken the boys and moved to the home of one of her relatives. She had felt strong evil presences in her home, especially in a back bedroom and especially in the closet of that back bedroom.

The backstory to this situation is that there is much evidence that her boyfriend (not my son) had worked spells within the apartment. Another friend of hers had also felt this dark presence and had become so frightened that he had not returned to visit after that experience.

She had told me that the person casting these spells was a person who was practicing the Rastafarian religion which is a system that believes in various types of acts designed to manipulate people by placing those people under their spell by working roots, killing chickens, and other modes of witchcraft.

It was a Saturday night when I used the key that she had left me and unlocked the apartment door and entered. Or at least, I *tried* to enter but was immediately met with an invisible force so strongly pressing against my chest with an obvious effort to prevent my entry. I had my Bible with me and had prayed in advance of my arrival. I not only had my Bible but also my anointing oil and a cloth that I had anointed with oil. As I pushed my way (by loudly praying and pleading the blood of Jesus Christ) forward against the dark energy, I began to anoint all the entry/exist parts of the apartment—windows and doors. As I did so, I was strongly and loudly citing Scripture and telling the demon or demons that they are defeated by the shed blood of Jesus Christ and that they have to go.

As I walked closer and closer to the back bedroom, the push-back was overwhelming. I was afraid, but I was not going to give up and leave. I was determined to be the instrument of the Holy Spirit to allow his presence to overpower the evil presence. I read several portions of Scripture as I inched my way closer and closer to the back closet of that bedroom. I was barely able to reach the closet door and open it, but when I did so, I tossed the anointed cloth inside of it. Right after I did that, as I continued to plead the blood of Christ against the satanic forces, I felt a rush of cold air breeze over my left shoulder and exit the nearby window.

There was a sudden rush of wind outside. At the same time, there was a sudden sense of peace within the home. There was no more heaviness or pushback. There was peace. I left as I continued to speak words of blessing over the apartment, closing the door and locking it.

I called my ex-daughter-in-law and told her that her apartment was now a place of peace, and she could move back in. She did so a couple of days later, and she immediately verified that there was no more heaviness or darkness inside.

*****

A few years later, perhaps closer to 2010 or thereabouts, a life-long friend of mine called me and asked me to pray over the home where one of her sons and his wife lived. She also stated that the place seemed evil, and darkness prevailed within it. When I arrived at the home and was welcomed in, I felt that same resistance pushing against me. The couple had a dog who was barking at me, so they put the dog outside. As I went from room to room, anointing the doors and windows, praying, and reciting Scripture, the couple were in the kitchen of the home because they wanted to leave me alone to perform my tasks of asking the Lord to remove the evil from the house.

At the moment, when I felt that darkness leave, there was a simultaneous rush of wind outside the house, and the dog started barking furiously and frighteningly. But in a few moments, all was calm inside and outside. The couple thanked me profusely. I thanked God profusely. Then I left. I heard from my friend that her son and wife reported to her that they felt a distinct difference in their home after that.

Prayer, a Committee Meeting, and a Well-Placed Empty Seat, 2005

The steps of a good man are ordered by the
Lord, and he delighteth in his way.

—Psalms 37:23

In January 1973, I left the church my father pastored and became of member of the Church of the Open Door in Elyria, Ohio. The details behind that decision are not pertinent to this book.

In May of 2005, I had been one of the members of the Church of the Open Door's life board under the leadership of Pastor David Walls for a few years. The board was scheduled to have its meeting after Sunday morning worship service that particular Sunday in May. For some reason, I was a bit later than normal arriving for the meeting. It had not yet begun, but by the time I arrived, there was one seat directly in front of me as I entered the conference room, so I sat there.

A conversation began between a man to my left and a man to my right. The man to my left asked the man to my right what he planned to do with his house in Oberlin now that the gentleman and his wife, Darrell and Karen Carter, were planning to leave for the mission field. They had to decide how to handle the status of their house.

Darrell responded that he and Karen were considering renting it out. I heard that conversation and, the next day, called Darrell and nervously asked him more about that rental possibility. He and Karen invited me for dinner a few days later to discuss the matter. I told them I appreciated their hospitality but apologized because I most likely would not be financially able to meet both the first month and deposit requirement that is typically expected for renting. Even though my income was good, I had a lot of bills at that time in my life.

They immediately responded that because they knew and respected me, they would waive the deposit requirement. I couldn't believe my ears! They, then, made arrangements that we would meet again for further discussion at a point when they learned more about their departure date for the mission field.

However, when we did meet again, they had a different idea. They had decided to sell the house rather than renting it. They didn't want to be long-distance landlords. They wanted to be free to focus on their work as missionaries. Of course, that made sense, but my heart sank. If I hadn't been able to afford both first month rent and deposit, I most assuredly couldn't afford a 20 percent down payment on a house!

Upon telling them that, they said it needn't be that difficult. They explained ways in which they would be willing to work with me to accomplish the goal. They did exactly that.

The reason I was interested in buying a house is because the only house that I had ever enjoyed was the one my husband had purchased in 1969 or 1970, but it was foreclosed in 1972 due to his gambling and drinking addictions. So now, decades later, I felt that my dream would never be realized. I had had decades of setbacks early in my adult life, so I had never imagined being a homeowner again. I had always envied couples who had worked together and saved enough monies to pay a hefty down payment on a home while they were still only in their twenties or thirties.

But in October 2005, I became the owner of the blue house at 170 Jones Street. Over the years, I remodeled it in major ways and made it my own. Those of you who have been there can testify to the before and after of its nuances. I moved there from having lived in Crossings Village in Westlake since 1997. I loved Westlake, but it still wasn't a house. The apartments I lived in were lovely, but they weren't a house. So when my lease ended at Crossings Village, Darrell and Karen were not yet moved out due to certain delays here and there in their plans to move to their mission field. This left me with a month where I had nowhere to live.

At that time, I was teaching the Sunday school women's group at Church of the Open Door. The class was known as CAMEO which stands for "Come And Meet Each Other." One of the ladies in the class, Pat Kelly, offered her and her husband, Tim's, home for me to reside in until the house was ready in Oberlin. We have been fast friends ever since. During all the years I lived in the Oberlin house, Tim was my Mr. Fix-It. He was highly instrumental in the major remodeling projects.

My prayer and heart's desire to own a house again was realized when I moved into 170 Jones Street on October 4, 2005.

What Satan Means for Evil, God Means for Good, 2016

But as for you, ye thought evil against me;
but God meant it unto good.

—Genesis 50:20a

L eading into the spring semester of 2016, my teaching assign-
ments were fewer in number than typical. My financial obligations simply outweighed my potential income. As an adjunct professor, one does not have an annual salary. One is paid according to how
many credit hours they teach. Insult to injury, right about that same
time, I fell prey to an internet dating site scam that ultimately cost
me $8,000. At some point after that, I was scammed again on eBay
to the tune of $3,500. I was broke and embarrassed.

These crises led me to place a "For Sale" sign in my front yard
in the spring of 2016. Ultimately, however, selling the house immediately was not God's plan. His plan was for me to lease it, instead,
to a nice lady who had just been hired by the Oberlin Conservatory
of Music (affectionately called The Con). She had previously been
at the Cleveland Institute of Music. My next-door neighbor was an
administrative associate at The Con who received a call from this
lady whose first day at work was just a couple weeks or so away. The
new hire wanted to know from my neighbor if she knew of any available, reasonably priced houses in Oberlin. My neighbor immediately
told her about my house.

Upon interviewing with this lady from Cleveland and her two children and upon obtaining three stellar letters of recommendation, she asked me if I would consider a lease instead of doing an immediate sale. For one reason, there would simply not be enough time for the sale process. I agreed because I also needed to be moved into the apartment that I had found on the same date that she needed to have her first day at The Con.

When I told her what I would charge her for rent, she initially said okay, but the next day, she called and asked me if I was absolutely *sure* that that amount was what I *really* wanted to ask. She said she thought the house was worth more than that monthly rental charge, especially because I had had to leave a lot of my furniture and new kitchen appliances there. My apartment would not hold five bedrooms of furniture, plus a living room, family room, and eat-in kitchen.

I was amazed at her honesty! I increased the monthly rent cost by another $150, and she still was pleased. I actually learned later through various knowledgeable sources that I could have easily asked for and received another $150 to $650 more! Anyway, I did not increase it when I found this out. She received a blessing from it, but so did I. My situation has steadily improved over these three years to 2019 as I am writing this book, and I feel blessed—so blessed!

I needed the three-year lease income in order to supplement my other income. I sold the house to her on July 31, 2019. I am in a much better financial condition, having done it this way—God's way!

Now, I am in the process of moving in the direction of purchasing a house after my apartment lease expires on June 30, 2020. I have asked the Lord for what I need and desire in a home and all the reasons why I need and desire that kind of a house.

Several people have inquired as to why I want to go from an apartment to a bigger house at my age. The answer is simple. I have done everything later in life than what is normal for my age. After all, I didn't start college until I was forty-one years old. I didn't have my own house as a single divorced woman until I was sixty-one years old. I am doing things in life twenty-five years later than people my age because I started seeing my dreams coming true twenty-five years later than normal.

Another example of doing things later than the norm is that my very best friend, Jackie Fleet, is someone whom I met during her first semester at Oberlin and my third semester there. She was seventeen and I was forty-two. She and I locked eyes in the Psychology class, as the result of something the professor said that impacted each of us. We did not know each other at that point. We had never had a single conversation, but there was something about how our eyes locked in a mutual response to what the professor had just said that caused us to introduce ourselves to one another right after that class.

She and I have lived very parallel lives ever since, in terms of our faith and values, our marriages and the dynamics therein, our children and their dynamics, and to some extent, our jobs. In no way do I feel my age, in spite of some health crises that I have experienced during the last couple of decades. My spirit is still young, and my dreams are still being dreamt.

Movie Theater Manager Allows Prayer Circle, 2015 and Beyond

For we walk by faith, and not by sight.

—2 Corinthians 5:7

*Faith is the substance of things hoped for, and
the evidence of things not seen.*

—Hebrews 11:1

Several very good faith-based movies have been produced in this decade of the 2010s. I highly appreciated many of them, including *Courageous, Fireproof, War Room, God's Not Dead, God's Not Dead 2, Unbroken, The Shack,* and many more. It occurred to me that a way of witnessing to people who do not know Jesus as their Savior and Lord would be to do so in the movie theater.

Now, that was a "foolish" idea, I thought. I knew that I couldn't just start doing such an "irrational" thing. I would likely be kicked out of the theater by the management, so I laid that idea aside. However, the idea didn't leave me alone. Weeks went by, and I continued to be pressured (yet again!) by the Holy Spirit to go to the Cobblestone Regal Cinema in the nearby town of Sheffield and ask to speak to the manager. Of course, I was nervous while standing in the lobby awaiting him.

I explained to him what I wanted to do and how it would be done discreetly and without any interference to patrons who would not be interested. I explained that it would not be loud or disruptive in any way. I also said that it would be brief. Finally, I explained that I would make moviegoers aware of this plan by standing at the door of the room where the movie would be showing and would hand out invitations to entering patrons. I would tell them that the invitation was an explanation of a brief event that would be happening right outside the viewing room right after the movie ends, and if they are interested in joining, the event will not take more than five or ten minutes of their time.

The very first prayer circle had about twenty-five people in it. We all joined hands, and I prayed a prayer of thanks to the Lord for leading movie producers to produce these kinds of movies. I also prayed that people who come but who do not yet know the Lord as Savior would be touched by the message of these films. A few others in the circle also chose to pray. The movie that night had been about a little boy who had died and gone to heaven but then returned to tell about his experience.

Interestingly, the day that I had nervously walked into the theater and spoke to the manager, who had smiled and said yes, I found out later that he is a Christian! The largest crowd happened on a Saturday night after watching *God's Not Dead 2*. There was a total of seventy-one people who joined the *Reel-to-Real Prayer Circle* that night!

The crowd was so big that concentric circles were formed in order to not block the hallway of other patrons needing to pass by! Security guards had obviously come over to see what the big crowd was all about, but I had not seen them do so because we were all praying. I figured out that the guards had come over because as the crowd was dispersing and leaving and I was walking past the manager's podium also leaving, the guards and the manager were smiling at me!

The rest of this story is that after the manager at Cobblestone had granted me the opportunity to do the prayer circles there (later named *The Reel-to-Real Prayer Circle*, and whose Scripture motto was 2 Chronicles 7:14, all of which was placed onto T-shirts I had designed), I got up the courage to drive over to the Crocker Park Regal Cinema and asked that manager the same request. He also said yes. However, his yes was not as ready and open as was the manager at Sheffield. Furthermore, it turned out that the layout of the Westlake theater was not physically as "user-friendly" for doing this, but the layout of the Sheffield theater was perfect for it! It allowed me to convene the circles right outside the showing room in the hallway, not in the main lobby. This theater was the one within Holy Spirit's plan.

I have not done any of these events since 2017 due to my tight academic schedule, working on my doctoral degree, but it was a real blessing for the span of time that it was meant to last. One of the people in the crowd of seventy-one people that Saturday night was so blessed by the event that she asked me if she could put a picture of the praying crowd on Facebook, and I agreed. When I got home that Saturday night, she had already posted it!

Food, Friends, Faculty, and a Faculty Atheist, Early to Mid-2019

*Blessed is the man that walketh not in the counsel of
the ungodly… His delight is in the law of the Lord,
and in his law doth he meditate day and night.*

—Psalms 1:1a–2

*Whatsoever things are true, whatsoever things are honest,
whatsoever things are just, whatsoever things are pure,
whatsoever things are lovely, whatsoever things are of good report;
if there be any virtue, and if there be any praise, think on these things.*

—Philippians 4:8

It was a Sunday afternoon after church, and I was at one of my favorite restaurants, Carrabba's. The pastor had preached a powerful sermon, and I was in great spirits. Often, I go to this restaurant after church service. I know many of the servers by name, and they know me. The Holy Spirit started "pushing" me yet again! This time, He told me to ask a couple of those servers if there was anything that I could pray for on their behalf. Jake looked surprised and smiled, stating that he appreciated the question, but he could think of nothing specific at that moment, so I promised to just pray a general prayer on his behalf. He went on about his duties as I silently talked to the Lord on Jake's behalf.

There is a backstory to why I did this. I must give credit to the missionary couple, Darrell and Karen Carter, who had sold me the house and who are supported by our church. When they were back in Ohio on furlough, they had treated me, not too many weeks prior, to a meal at Carrabba's because they told me to select the restaurant of my choice because they just wanted to treat me to dinner. While we had been there, Darrell had asked our server if there was anything he could pray about on her behalf. He explained that *"we are Christians, and we love to pray for people. Is there anything we can pray about for you?"* The server looked pleasantly surprised and shared certain concerns, and then, we prayed discreetly and briefly for those needs.

It was during some relatively short period of days or weeks thereafter when I was there again, and that serving was working and saw me. She shared that the prayer had been heard because the situation had improved!

It is from that experience, as much as it as from the pastor's sermon, that I had the courage to ask my server friends if I could pray for them that particular Sunday after church. I did not ask every single server but only those that the Spirit told me to ask. I had never done it before nor again—so far. I only do what Holy Spirit tells me to do. It is scary enough to do it when He tells me to, let alone I should ever strike out on my own to do something so "ridiculous" and "scary" and "inappropriate."

Anyway, after talking to Jake and silently praying for him, Kay was the other one that I was led to. However, she did not come into close enough proximity for me to discreetly ask her the prayer question. As I saw glimpses of her while doing her job, I noticed that she looked to be pushing herself to keep pleasantness on her usually very pleasant face. She appeared either depressed, tired, or perhaps, ill. It was quite a noticeable difference. She never came close enough for me to ask her anything. The restaurant was quite busy that day.

However, as I had finished my meal and paid my server, Jake, I headed toward the door to leave, but Holy Spirit "pushed" me— again! He said that I should ask the person at the host stand if I may speak to Kay for a brief moment. They retrieved her from the kitchen where she was receiving a completed order. She came to me. I told her that I had noticed she did not appear to feel well but how I had admired her for trying hard to keep her professional face on.

I then said, "This will only take a couple seconds of your time, but I wonder if there is anything I can pray for on your behalf?"

She was so touched, and as the tears began to flow, she explained that she had been having awful migraine heads for about three weeks, and she had an upcoming doctor's appointment to be checked. I discreetly and quickly prayed specifically for her needs, said amen, and left. She had tears in her eyes and thanked me!

It was probably two or three weeks later when I returned, and she had a big smile! She said that shortly after the prayer, her headache diminished and soon disappeared! She thanked me profusely!

*****

Now, I will talk about two faculty peers of mine at LCCC. I saw one of them crying and being comforted by the administrative associate one day toward the ending of the spring 2019 semester. This was unusual. She was obviously distraught. When I directly asked her, she explained that she had just been diagnosed with melanoma and was scared. She further explained that she had won a previous battle with cancer and was devastated that it seemed to have returned.

She is a nice lady but not one with whom I have had a lot of interpersonal interaction. However, when she shared the news about the diagnosis, I asked her if I might be able to stop by her office later that day because there was a question that I would like to ask her. She looked only slightly confused but said yes. That afternoon, as she welcomed me into her office, I told her that I am a minister and that I believe in prayer. I never talk about my ministerial license, but I felt the need to add some "legitimacy" to the fact that I knew I was about to ask her if I could pray for her situation. I explained that I do often pray for people.

She responded that she had put her faith aside many years ago but that I could pray for her. I thanked her and reached across her desk as I sat across from her. I gestured for her to grasp my hands.

She did. I prayed audibly, specifically, but briefly. When I was finished, I noted that she had tears in her eyes. She repeated that even though she had put faith aside in her life, she just might call on me again to do that again! I left her office and was scared to death about how she would treat me in the future! She is a PhD tenured professor, after all!

Silly me, no need for fear. Perfect love casts out fear. Instead, she has updated me a couple of times since then about how she is doing, including a surgical procedure. She reported that she is doing well, though I do not know if that means remission or not.

*****

There was another faculty member who passed away a few months ago whom the Holy Spirit "made me" say something to when it was still last spring semester 2019. He had a decades-long history of being an absolute atheist who would try to get all of students to get rid of their faith. He made it crystal clear that he did not believe in God and neither should they. After all, his point was that education and "superstition" don't mix!

Insult to injury, this man was not very well-liked by many of his peers because he was generally very pompous, argumentative, and narcissistic. He had been one among the first faculty hired by LCCC in its early days of the 1960s or 1970s, probably becoming the most senior faculty member in recent decades.

This man did not speak to me when I would greet him from the time that I began teaching there in 2004. However, after a few such snubs, I refused to let him continue to treat me so subserviently, arrogantly, and rudely. So the time came when I greeted him, I would stop to wait for a return greeting. When I did not get it, I would just stand there and repeat my greeting to him and wait for an appropriate response. He gave it. He was not used to such boldness. I was supposed to be shaking in my boots.

Early in the beginning of the spring semester, I was walking from my car toward the building, and he was headed toward his awaiting vehicle with his wife behind the wheel. That morning, before I had arrived at work, I had asked the Lord to send me across the path of someone whom I could pray for. Well, I didn't expect it to be this man, but the Lord wanted it to be this man!

So as the Lord would have it, I approached this man at a most "convenient" vantage point wherein I could not only greet him but also say to him, "Hello, John [pseudonym], I just want you to know that I am praying for you."

He stopped and turned and looked right into my face, his eyes widened in surprise. Then, he responded, "Thank you, why…thank you very much!"

I was so nervous, but I held strong and responded, "You're welcome [John]! I just wanted you to know that!" Whew! My heart was pounding as I turned and walked on into the building! But to ensure that I had not lied to John, I did pray for him (his salvation and health needs) as I walked toward the office space within which he and I worked.

Before he died in or about October 2019, I wondered if he heard the prompting of the Holy Spirit in his heart. We shall see. I'm sure he didn't forget my words of assurance that he was being prayed for, especially because those words of assurance were uttered by one of his educated colleagues who had also stood up to his gruffness over the years!

*****

Finally, a fellow faculty member, whom I did not have a relationship with and hardly ever saw, approached me early in the spring semester 2019, and we exchanged brief greetings. This lady never seemed happy to me during the few times I did see her. Several interactions between us eventually led to her asking if she and I could have lunch together, off campus, sometime. In those previous interactions, she had clearly learned about my faith, peace, joy, and love. She acknowledged that she was intrigued and interested in learning more about all of that.

This whole relationship began one morning after I had (again) asked the Lord to guide my steps and bring someone across my path that I could show the love of Christ to them or impact their life in some way. Well, I should have learned by now to be careful of what I pray for. But apparently, I haven't learned that yet!

As a result, as I was getting out of my car and heading toward the building, so was she and her husband. They ended up actually a little ahead of me. I noticed that her husband—whom I did not know at that time was her husband—kept walking into a different direction rather than heading toward the building. Later that day, when she struck up a conversation with me and was commenting on something that had changed about my appearance, we ultimately began to learn a little about each other.

In the process, I learned that the gentleman whom she said was her husband had kept walking that morning because he liked to go on "prayer walks" around the campus and did so regularly! Oh boy, okay, Lord, it looks like you are opening yet another door here for me to walk through! You are answering that morning prayer requesting that you bring someone across my path that I can witness to! Well, I walked through that open door and several conversations ensued over the course of the whole spring semester!

She shared personal family issues with me for which I always prayed. She said that she had never met anyone like me who had such faith. She, then, issued the invitation to have lunch together off campus on our free time. Ultimately, we agreed on lunch at Lorenzo's Pizzeria in Oberlin. She had invited her husband to join us, but he only brought her and then busied himself elsewhere while she and I spent the hour together. She was touched by my audible, direct, hand-grasping prayer wherein I thanked God for our food. As always, I did so briefly and with discretion, never trying to bring negative attention to myself or those with me.

As always, when I finished, she was tearing up and saying that she had never heard anyone do that kind of praying and that she wished she could do that! I had learned many weeks or months before that late-semester day that she and her husband are from a more ritualistic, less Bible-centered faith tradition which does not espouse the kind of raw and direct praying style that I used.

Nevertheless, when the end of the semester of spring 2019 came, she asked me what my teaching schedule would be for the summer because she hoped our paths would cross again. It turned out that they did not nor did they during the fall 2019 semester.

I Waited Thirty-Five Years for this, December 2019!

Pray without ceasing.

—2 Corinthians 5:17

Sorry ya'll, this one is strictly between me and God! My phone rang today, December 17, and for two hours, the voice on the other end was the source of answering thirty-five years of my persistent, often faith-filled, but sometimes, shaky, scared, and even doubting prayer! Don't even try to guess what I'm talking about. You'll probably be wrong! All I can say right now is, "Thank you, *Jesus!*"

More Answers Are Also on Their Way, 2019 and Forward

*Ask and it shall be given you, seek and ye shall find,
knock, and it shall be opened unto you.*

—Matthew 7:7

Moving forward, here are some major things that I am asking the Lord for, but I will and should receive them only if he also wants them for me:

1. some very important people in my life whom I'm praying for that they accept the Lord as their Savior;
2. That I get my new house in 2020;
3. That I will earn my doctoral degree in community care and pastoral counseling in 2020 or no later than 2021;
4. That I get to take my first ever *for real* vacation of my life in 2021 which will be either a cruise or a trip to the holy land; and finally
5. That some other important people whom I do not yet know will be led to the Lord because the Holy Spirit will use me to do it. Yes, use me, Lord, use me until you use me up!

SAMMY DAVIS-DYSON strikes a triumphant pose after receiving her degree at Oberlin College Monday.

Elyria mom, 45, climbs mountains to reach top

By CAROLYN PIONE
C-T Staff Writer

OBERLIN — Sammie Davis-Dobson gets angry when she hears people claim

dren while taking a full load of courses and graduating in four years.

"As a result of all that has happened in my life, I can

Sammie Davis-Dyson

The Elyria Chronicle Telegram article (though filled with several errors, including the statement that I was from Elyria—even though I was actually from Oberlin) was titled "*Elyria mom, 45, climbs mountains to reach the top*". It was published Tuesday, May 29th, 1990, by staff writer Carolyn Pione who writes (in part):

> *Davis Dyson's efficiency allowed her to raise her three children…as well as start a student organization, be elected alumni vice president of her graduating class, and maintain about a B-plus average with a double major in psychology and religion.*
>
> *Through the campus organization she founded, Minority Students for Careers in Higher Education, Davis-Dyson hopes to see more blacks [enter] graduate school [beyond the undergraduate (Bachelor degree) level].*
>
> *"When my brothers and I got past [my parents' education level, they encouraged us", she said. "We heard the words echoing in our minds, 'Hey, don't stop', and that encouraged us."*

The Oberlin News-Tribune titled their article *"Grad turns under-privileged to well-educated"*. It was published Tuesday, June 5th, by staff writer Tom Corrigan. Some of his excerpts include:

> *"Thank God I was naïve", says Oberlin's Sammie Davis-Dyson of her first day back to the classroom after 24 years. "If I had really known what to expect, I would've chickened out."*
>
> *After four years of "riding through waves of shock", struggling through classes (as a double major student, no less), juggling study time with raising three children by herself, singing in two different choirs, still finding time to become the founder of a new and one-of-a-kind student organization and getting herself elected her class vice president, Davis-Dyson, 45, was among the 782 students who graduated May 28 from Oberlin College.*
>
> *In 1987, she was the recipient of a National Outstanding College Student of America award.*
>
> *Quite a change for a woman who four years ago nearly fit the stereotypical picture many of us conjure up when we hear the term "underprivileged": a divorced mother, a minority, unemployed, living on public assistance in public housing. At the time she started her approximately $21,000-a-year education, she was officially living below the poverty level.*

The Lorain Morning Journal also wrote an article about the graduation, but I was unable to find it in their archives.

About the Author

S ammie has had life experiences that have spanned times of despair, fear, emotional, and psychological pain. She has also experienced many times of surprising transformations and providential interventions from Holy Spirit himself!

She has experienced God's discipline many times as her disobedience required such discipline. She learned from it—big time! It is her desire now to share her life with those who have lost hope or feel that their prayers go no higher "than the ceiling".

She wants you to know that as you learn to walk in submission and obedience, Holy Spirit becomes free to heap blessings upon you, in good measure, pressed down, shaken together, and running over! (Luke 6:38)